MW00351975

EXPERIMENT 116

USING ELECTRICITY

Series Editor, Nick Montfort

Using Electricity is a series of computer generated books, meant to actually reward reading in conventional and unconventional ways. The series title takes a line from the computer generated poem "A House of Dust," developed by Alison Knowles with James Tenney in 1967. This work, a FORTRAN computer program and a significant early generator of poetic text, combines different lines to produce descriptions of houses.

R E N A J . M O S T E I R I N

EXPERIMENT 116

Counterpath
Denver
2022

Counterpath
Denver, Colorado
www.counterpathpress.org

© 2022 Rena J. Mosteirin. All rights reserved.

Library of Congress Cataloging in Publication Data is available.

ISBN 978-1-93-399676-9 (paperback)

CONTENTS

Let me go to the right spirits to get married
Stop it. For love does not love
Whenever changing
Or keep it off for the transfer.
Oh! This is brighter silence
He looks like storms and burnt again;
It's everywhere,
Uniquely unknown, but how much is that right?
For the love is foolish, even though the dogs and the spirits
He goes to the patient's illness;
Evolution has not changed shortly for hours and weeks,
But it is because it's dirty.
If it's a mistake and I'm guilty
I have never been written, ever loved someone.

Let me not marry true spirit
Admit obstruction. Love is not love
What does it change when the change gets,
Or bend with the suppressor to remove it.
Oh no! it is still a fixed brand
This watch the storms and never shake;
He is the star of every rod crust,
Its value is unknown, although its height is taken.
Love is not foolish in times, even if her lips and cheeks are pink
Inside the indigo folding compass is;
Love does not change by its short hours and weeks,
But it brings him to the limits of fatality.
If this is a mistake and I try,
I never write, nor does anyone ever love it.

Do not leave me the marriage of the true spirit
Acknowledge obstacles. Love is not love
Who changes when he finds a change,
Or bend with a nail polish remover to remove.
Haiwa! the bullet is always fixed
It looks at the storm and will never be shaken;
It is the star of all magic wand bark,
Its value is unknown, although its size is determined.
Love is not a fool of the weather, even the lips and cheeks are loud
In his comfy bow the sect is coming;
Love does not change with its short hours and weeks,
But it does strengthen itself even in the face of danger.
If there is error in me and I see it,
I never wrote, or any man ever wanted.

Don't marry me with real minds
Recognize obstacles. Love is not love
What changes when it changes
Or bend with a remover.
Oh no! it is always a fixed mark
He looks at the storms and never shakes them;
A star is a stick for every bark,
Whose value is not known, although the height is covered.
Love is not a silly time, despite its pink lips and cheeks
His sickle compass is folded into it;
Love does not change with short hours and weeks,
But he also confirms this on the verge of conviction.
If this is a mistake and I have proved it,
I never wrote it, and no one loved it.

Don't leave me for a true heart marriage
Acknowledge the obstacle. Love is not love
Change when it is found
Or fold it with a remover to remove it.
Ohno! It's always a fixed brand
No one is moved by the sight of the storm;
The bark star of each magic wand,
Its height is retrieved, but its value is unknown.
Has rosy lips and cheeks, but love is not stupid
They come inside the folding sickle compass.
Love does not change in that short time and week,
But it makes it to the brink of ruin.
If this was mistakenly caused to me,
I had never written it and no one loved it.

→ **MAORI** → **LATIN** →

You involve me call is not true marriage memories
Take the left subnavigation +. Love is not love
What will be different when it is seen,
Bend and pull to remove.
Oh! The permanent sign
The face of weather or of open, however,
This they learn all the hills were the star.
It must also be detected height.
Love is stupid, that is, without cause and lip
There is no cover in explosive;
Self is nothing short weeks to hours;
But it has the purpose of the sentence.
If this is a mistake to say that I die
He who loved me, and I can not write.

That doesn't make me almost smart
Accept problems. Jesus is not love
What changes when the change occurs,
Or double with a remover to remove.
No! it is a positive sign
It looks cloudy and does not tremble;
A star for every bitterness,
The value is unknown, although its height will be taken into account.
The sauna is not crazy, although the lips are sweet and cheeky
In the compass came loose blades;
The measure does not change with its short hours and weeks,
But it brought him to the brink of destruction.
If this is a mistake and it presents itself to me,
I never wrote and no one ever loved me.

Let me not marry the true spirit
Accept obstacles. Love is not love
What changes when there is a change
Or hang with a remover to remove.
Oh no! This is a constant signal.
She looked at temptation and never wavered.
It is the star for every lost shell.
Who is valuable is not yet known, but they take his height.
Love is not a fool of time Pink lips and cheeks
Comes in the compass of his curved worm;
Love does not change in its short and weeks.
But it dries to death.
If this is a mistake and we want to produce
I have never written and no one likes it.

Do not allow me to marry sensibly
Allow lanes. Love is not love
What will change when there is a change,
Τα bows and can be moved.
Alas! it is a permanent sign
This is like a storm that will not shake.
He is the star of every tree.
Who is unworthy to be known, while taking his height.
Love is not foolish at all, even on the lips and cheeks
Comes in the pocket of a castle knife.
Love does not change with its short hours and weeks,
But it takes the edge of the end.
If this is wrong do not convince me.
I do not write, no one loves.

Do not marry the true senses.
Accept obstacles Love is not love
Which will change when changes are found
Or bend it with a solution to remove it.
No! It is a brand that is permanent.
Look at the storm and not be moved.
It is the star of all kinds of magical bark.
The value of anyone is unknown even if his height is taken.
Love is not the stupid thing of time. But are bloody lips and cheeks.
Within the compass cut at his bend.
Love doesn't change over the short hours and weeks.
But brought it to the brink of punishment.
If this is wrong and I have proven
I have never written and have never been loved.

Let me not have a real marriage
Acknowledge obstacles. Love is not love
Find out what changes are changing,
Or bend it with a remover to remove it.
Oh no! This is a permanent sign
It looks stormy and will never waver.
It's the star of every stick skin,
Although he is tall, it is still not clear who is worth it.
Love is not a fool of time, despite its rosy lips and cheeks
The compass of his curved sickle struck.
Love will not change with his short time and weeks,
But even on the brink of collapse, it must be proven.
If this is wrong and I prove it,
I've never written a book and no one likes it.

Do not let me marry real minds
Accept barriers. Love is not love
That changes when it finds change,
Or comb with the remover to remove it.
Oh no! It is an established sign forever
Which looks in temples and is never shaken;
It is the star of every wand,
It is not known who it is worth, although the height will be taken.
Fool loves no time, though with pink lips and cheeks
Inside the campus the sequence descends;
Love does not change with his short hours and weeks,
But carry it even to the brink of injury.
If this is a mistake and I'm convinced,
I never wrote, and no one ever lov'd.

Let me not go to the wedding of real minds
Accept crisis. Love is not love
Which changes when it changes,
Or love a remover to remove.
Oh no! This is a permanent sign
It looks at mistakes and does not go down.
A star among all the stars that were made,
Its value is unknown, although its height was taken.
Love is not the foolishness of time, though pink lips and cheeks
Her mother comes to the midwife's knees.
Love does not change with its short hours and weeks,
But there is also the end of suffering.
If it is a mistake and I have it.
I never write, and no one loves me anymore.

Let us not marry with true thoughts
Obtain obstacles. Love is not love
That changes when change occurs,
Or bend with the remover to remove.
Oh no! it is a firm mark forever
That looks to temples and is never shaken;
It is the star of every lost bark,
Unknown who is worthy, though his height is taken.
Love crazy no Time, though rosy lips and cheeks
Inside the compass of the curved sickle;
Love does not change with its short hours and weeks,
But bring it even to the edge of doom.
If this is a mistake and in my experience,
I have never written, nor anyone who has ever loved.

We will not marry with a right heart
Acknowledge your disability. Love is not love
That changes when change is discovered
Or bend it with a remover to remove.
No! It is always a constant signal
He sees the storm and does not shake.
She is the star of every cane ring shell.
Its height is unacceptable, but no one knows its merit.
Love is not a fool of time, but rosy lips and cheeks
In the compass of the curved crescent
Love does not change in its short and prime time.
But it will last until the end of destiny.
If this is a mistake and I prove it
I didn't write, and I didn't love anyone.

Don't let me have a real marriage mind
Admit your barriers. Love is not love
Who changes when he sees change
Or bend it with a remover to remove.
Oh no! it is always a fixed sign
It looks at storms and never hesitates;
He is the star of every barking wand
Its value is unknown, although its height is taken.
Love is not stupid in Time, even if the lips and cheeks are pink
Inside his bent crescent-shaped compass;
Love does not change in its short hours and weeks
But he still carries it to the brink of extinction.
If it was a mistake and it proved to me
I have never written, not even any person I loved.

Don't marry with a real mind
Recognition of barriers. Love is not love
It changes as you change,
Or use a cleanser to get rid of it.
Or not! This is definitely a sign
Who will see the storm and not tremble;
He is the star in every lost tree,
Although the height is taken, this value is not known.
Although lips and cheeks are floral, love is sometimes not stupid
Let's get to the complex harvesting complex;
Love hours and weeks do not change,
But he also survived at the end of his life.
If this is not true and is proven,
I never write, and there are no other people I love.

Do not let me get married in a real marriage
Recognize challenges. Love is not
What changes when changed,
Or bend with medicine to remove it.
Oh no! it is a still fixed point
It was like a storm and never trembled;
This is the star of every wall;
The price is uncertain, no matter how long.
Love is not a foolish time, even if it hurts your cheek and cheek
In his bow the sickle bow;
Love does not change with its short weeks and weeks,
But carry it out on the brink of damage.
If he is wrong and asks me,
I have never written before, and no one loves.

→ CORSICAN → MACEDONIAN →

Do not leave me to the marriage of true minds
He acknowledges obstacles. Love is not love
What changes when change is found,
Or fold it with the remover to remove it.
Oh no! is always a fixed brand
He sees the storms and never shakes;
It's a star on every wand,
For what value it is unknown, although its height will be taken.
Love is not the smell of time, even if the lips and cheeks are pink
Inside his folded sickle compass comes;
Love does not change with its short hours and weeks,
But it also brings him to the brink of condemnation.
If this is a mistake and try it with me,
I have never written, nor has anyone ever wanted to.

Let me not marry with real thoughts
Acknowledge the obstacle. Love is not love
Change when you see change,
Or lean the puller to remove it.
Or not! it is a sign that always heals
It looks turbulent and motionless;
It's the star of all the ships on the ship,
Its unknown value, even if you take its height.
Love is not a stupid time, even pink lips and cheeks
Inside the compass enters his twisted sword;
Love never changes in its short hours and weeks,
Although it was brought to the brink of destruction.
If this is also wrong, in my opinion,
I never wrote and no one loves me.

→ KINYARWANDA → MALAY →

Let me not get married in real mind
Accept obstacles. Love is not love
What happens when it changes,
Or bend and pull out.
No! it is a permanent sign
That hangs in the wind and you will not be shaken;
Stars for every magic wand bark,
Who has an unknown value, even if its height is taken into account.
Love does not deceive now, even the lips of the cheeks
On his compass he lowered his sickle;
Love does not change for hours and weeks,
But he survived on the threshold of adversity.
If this is a mistake and for me to prove it,
I never wrote, no one liked it.

Talk about real ideas marriage
Accept the obstacles. Love is not love
Which will change when there is a change,
Or bend over to remove it.
No, it is a permanent sign
He sees the storms ‡ never shakes.
It is a star for every traveler
Despite its height, whose value is unknown?
Love is not a fool of time, despite the purple lips and cheeks
It comes with its flexible hook compass.
Love does not change in a matter of hours.
But even on the brink of falling.
If this is a mistake, then it has been confirmed to me,
I will never write, no one will ever like.

I should not be in a marriage of true minds
Accepting restrictions. Love is not love
What changes as the changes become available,
Or bend to the giver to remove.
Oh no! It is a permanent symbol
It looks over the storm and never shakes;
It's a star for every moving bark,
Its value is unknown, although its length will take.
Love is not a fool of time, though the lips and cheeks are sweet
As part of his vision to buy a sickle to come;
Love changes not only in its short hours and weeks,
But it bears fruit even on the verge of punishment.
If this is a mistake and it has been verified,
I never wrote, and no one ever liked it.

Don't let me enter a marriage of true souls
Acknowledge the obstacles. Love is not love
What changes when change is found,
Or bend with detergent to remove.
Oh no! it is always a permanent imprint
It looks like a storm and never shakes;
It is a star for every shell of a stick,
Whose value is unknown, although its height is taken.
Love is not a deception of time, even with rosy lips and cheeks
Inside his bent compass;
Love does not change with its short hour and week,
But it persisted to the end of ruin.
If this is a mistake and if I deliver,
I have never written, nor do anyone like it.

Let me love you
Add hiccups. Love is not love
Which changes when we see this change,
Or type with subtraction.
Oh! This is a sign that is marked forever
He looks at the temples and does not move;
It is the star of every moving tree,
The value of which is unknown, although its height is taken.
The moment of love is not foolish, although the lips and cheeks are thick
Within the compass it is repaired;
Do not fall in love with your short time and weeks,
But he endured it to the point of destruction.
If it is wrong and will show me,
I do not write, nor do we love any man at all.

The real reason is don't let me at the wedding
Identify problems. Love is not love
What changes when change occurs
Or bend and remove the stripper.
Anyway! This is a permanent sign
The wind blows and it always shakes;
The star disappeared in the whole sky,
Despite his high status, who needs to know.
Despite red lips and cheeks, love is not the folly of time
He comes out on the compass of his parish;
Love changes in less hours and weeks,
But it will also be tested to the end.
If this error prompts you,
I don't write or love anyone.

→ SESOTHO → LATVIAN → LATIN →

It is not, however, enter into their minds in marriage,
Accept them. Love is not love
The change does not change when it comes to
Or will you be gone by the hand of the man's hand to move.
No other ätus! shape constant
It seems a tempest, shall not be moved;
I am a star out of it is diffused all the shadows,
Whether it is their own value, is unknowable, it can, however, in
    the stature of the launching.
The kiss of the time is not light love; not a spoon
Enter the turning circle and future
Love does not change brief hours and weeks;
But who endures until the destruction.
But if the error server submitted to me
I never wrote that no one ever liked it.

Don't let me into a real mind
Accept obstacles. Love is not love
It changes when it changes,
Or take a turn with the remover to remove.
Oh no! That is a definite sign
He watches the tests and never shakes;
He is the star of every wandering shell,
Whose value is unknown, yet its height is taken.
Love is not a foolish time despite having pink lips and cheeks
Its flexible hawk enters the compass;
Love does not change with its short hours and weeks,
But it also lasts until the brink of doom.
If this is a mistake and goes over to me,
I never write that no man wants.

→ LAO → UZBEK →

Don't marry me with a sincere heart
Accept the interruption. Love is not love
Which changes when you change,
Or bend to lift to lift.
Oh no! It's weird to be identified
He sees the storm and never shakes;
This is a star in every giant shell,
There is no value for a person who does not know even if his
    height is lowered.
Fools are not the fools of time, not even their lips and cheekbones
Weavers come to the compass of the world;
With its short hours and weeks, love does not change,
But raise it even to the level of damage.
If this is a mistake and follow me,
I never wrote and no one wrote.

It is not allowed to go to a real wedding
Accept the obstacles. Love is not love
Whatever changes,
In Removea, it bends with a separator to remove it.
No moon! This is a permanent sign
He looks at trials and never trembles.
The star of every crust,
It is unknown at this time what he will do after leaving the post.
Although the flower has lips and cheeks, love is not the stupidity of time
The compass of the bent sickle came;
Love does not change with its short hours and weeks,
Even before the penalty.
If it is a mistake and it depends on me
I never wrote a letter and no one loved me.

Don't let me marry you
Be aware of obstacles. Love is another love
That changed when this change was discovered,
Or curved and removed and removed.
Oh no! it is a permanent mark
He was seen in a storm and trembling;
This is the star of every mediator,
The advantage is unknown, although it can be considered high.
Love is not stupid Time, although the lips and cheeks are pink
On compass knife harvest twists and turns;
Love does not change in a few hours and weeks,
But even carry it to the end of the world.
If this is a mistake and I show it,
I never wrote, or that no one loved.

I shouldn't marry with the right thoughts
Accept the obstacles. Love is not love
What changes occur when changes are seen,
Or bend over with the eraser to erase.
Oh no! It's a sign that is always set
It watches the hurricane and never gets shaken;
This is a star for every stick bar,
Whose value is unknown, but height must be taken.
Lips and cheeks are rosy, although love is not the folly of time
His flexible crutch comes in the compass;
Love doesn't change with short hours and weeks,
But survived even to the point of destruction.
This is a mistake and if it seems to me
I have never written or loved anyone.

→ ODIA (ORIYA) → NORWEGIAN →

Do not give me a proper wedding
Accept the Restriction Love is not love
When it changes, it changes,
Or skewed with a remover for removal
Hello no! This is a permanent sign
It sees the vortex and never trembles;
It is the star of every wandering star,
Whose value is unknown, even if his height is taken
Love is not a fool, but pink lips and cheeks
Compassion comes within his humble prayer;
Love does not change with its short hours and weeks,
But it carries to the brink of destruction
If it turns out wrong and turns out for me,
I have never written or loved ever

Don't let me marry honestly
Accept obstacles. Love is not love
Change when you see a change
Or turn with the remover to remove.
not much. It is a symbol of eternity
It watches storms and never moves.
It is the star of every wandering.
His height has been taken, but his value is unknown.
Love is not the fool of time;
As it bends, it enters the blade's magnetic compass.
In a matter of weeks, love does not change.
But it is also accepted until the catastrophe.
If this is a mistake, forget me,
I never write, never love.

→ RUSSIAN → XHOSA →

Let me not marry a real intellectual marriage
Be aware of obstacles. Love is not love
What changes when these changes are found
Or wrapped with a pull-out drawer.
Oh no! it remains a fixed token
It looked at the storm and did not shake;
This is the star in the shell of all the magic rings
Its value is unknown, although its growth has been taken.
Love is not a mere figment of the imagination
Inside his curved ax, a compass came;
Love never changes with its hours and short weeks
But it is even resistant to death.
That is a mistake and I am sure
I didn't write and no one ever liked it.

I do not marry with true wisdom
Prano barriers. Love is not love
Which changes when you find out,
Or bend over with a lift.
Oh no! Always a stable brand
It is seen in the storm and never shakes
The star of every homeless skin,
It is unknown at this time what he will do after leaving the post.
Even though she had pink lips and cheeks, love was not stupid at the time
His bent papers come inside the compass.
Love does not change with its short time and week,
But keeps him on the brink of punishment.
If this is wrong and I have proof,
I never write, and no one wants to.

Let me not marry true minds
Recognize the limitations. Love is not love
Who changes when he finds a change
Or bend with a removable scraper.
Oh no! This is a permanent sign
He watches the storms and never vibrates;
He is the star of every wandering crust,
Its value is unknown, although its length is taken into account.
Love is not the fool of time, despite rosy lips and faces
It comes in the compass of its curved sickle;
Love doesn't change with its short hours and weeks,
But even take it to the brink of destruction.
If this is incorrect and I have to prove
I never wrote and no one liked it.

Allow a real mental marriage
Accept the challenges. Love is not love
Changes when changes are received,
Or foorarsada tools to copy looga.
Oh no! it is an eternal symbol
It looks at storms and never shakes;
He is the star of every desire.
Although their length is taken into account, their value is unknown.
Although lips and cheeks are soft, love is not a stupid time
The return point to the plow is approaching;
Love does not change short hours and weeks,
But take it to the edge of the heel.
If this is wrong and they blame me,
I never wrote, no one liked it.

Let me not marry real ideas
Accept the obstacles. Love is not love
When it changes, it changes,
Or curled up with a cleanser to remove.
Visual! This is a steady sign
One who looks at the storm and is not shaken.
This whole star is a moving skin
The value of the identity is unknown, although it is tall.
Love is not stupid, though its lips and cheeks are fine
Inside the campus, the cane is bent.
Love never changes in its few days,
But it can endure to the end.
If this is a mistake and it has been proven to me,
I don't write, and no one likes it.

I will not allow a sincere marriage
Accept the obstacles. Love is not love
When a modification is found, it changes
Or folded with a remover to remove.
Oh no! This is a constant brand
Look at the tests and never shake;
It is the star of each wand,
Nobody knows its value, despite its height.
Love is not foolish, although it has pink lips and cheeks
Enter your folding sickle's compass;
Love does not change with its brief hours and weeks,
But it is also on the verge of doom.
If this is a mistake and has been proven to me,
I never write, nor do I like any man.

Do not marry me with true wisdom
Acknowledge obstacles. Love is not love
When it changes, something that will change it,
Or bend with a scraper to remove.
Oh no! This is a constant sign
It shows strong winds and never trembles;
He is the star of every shell,
It is unknown at this time what he will do after leaving the post.
Despite having her pink lips and cheeks, love is not the folly of time
The compass of his wrapped ripper comes;
Love is not with her short hours and weeks
But he will carry it till the Day of Resurrection.
If it is wrong and is imposed on me,
I never wrote, no one loves.

Let me not marry real intellectuals
Accept the obstacle. Love is not love
Which changes when you find a change,
Or fold with a remover.
Oh no! it is a sign of eternity
It sees the storm and never shakes;
It is the star of every tree bark.
It is not clear whose value it is, but its height needs to be taken.
Pink lips and cheeks, but love is not the fool of Time
Inside the bending sickle comes his compass;
In his short hours and weeks, love does not change,
But he endures it to the brink of disaster.
If that was a mistake for me
I never wrote, no one loved me.

I don't let the real ones get married, of course
Accept clitis. Love is not love
Changes when changes are found
Or it is twisted with a remover to remove it.
What is it! "Fixed sign"
Faced with storms and never shaken;
He is in every star in the bark of the rod,
Despite his height, the value of which is unknown.
Love is not the stupidity of time, though pink lips and cheeks
It comes to the compass of a sloping mower;
Love does not change in short hours and weeks,
But it leads to doom.
If it's a mistake and it's proven to me
I never write, no man writes.

Don't leave me to a real marriage of mind
Accept the barriers. Love is not love
Which changes when you find out,
Or fold to remove.
Yes! it is a permanent firm brand
He looks at the storms and never shakes;
It's every shell star,
Even if its value is unknown, its height is taken.
Love is not the stupidity of time, even if it has lips and cheeks
Its sealed seal is inside the compass;
Love does not change with its short hours and weeks,
But take him to the edge of punishment.
If this is a mistake and it works,
I never wrote and no one liked it.

I will not be allowed to marry with a true heart
Acknowledge obstacles. Love is not love
What happens when he recognizes change,
Or bend with an eraser.
But no! It is still a strong brand
He looks at the storm and he never trembles;
He is the star of every wand shell,
The value of which is not known, must be taken.
Even with pink lips and cheeks, love is not the folly of time
In the compass of his bent sickle;
Love does not change with its short hours and weeks,
But it will continue until it becomes extinct.
And if this is wrong for me
I never write and never like anyone.

Don't leave me for a real mind marriage
Recognize the obstacles. Love is not love
When you find a change, change,
Or bend it with a remover and remove it.
Oh no! the brand is always stable
It looks at the storms and never shakes;
This star is for each rod shell,
Its value is unknown, although its height is taken.
Love isn't Zamona's weakness, though, with pink lips and cheeks
Inside the sickle compass;
Love doesn't change with your short hours and weeks,
But it can even lead to death.
If this is a mistake and intended for me,
I never wrote and no one ever loved me.

→ SINHALA → SLOVAK →

Don't let me marry a real mind
Accept the obstacles. Love is not love
What changes when a change is found
Or bend it with a remover.
Ojoj! It is a constant constant mark
He looks at the tests and never shakes.
He is the star of every book,
Its height should be taken, but its value is unknown.
Despite pink lips and cheeks, love is not Crazy
His flexible scythe comes to the compass;
Love does not change with its short hours and weeks,
However, it is on the verge of destruction.
If it's a mistake and it turns out to me,
I never wrote or loved anyone.

Not to marry a real mind
Accept barriers. Love is not love
Change when you see the change,
Or bend with a remover to remove it.
Not! it is a constant sign
He watches over the whirlwind and never trembles;
He is the star of all flying skins,
What is not known is unknown, although its height will be increased.
Love does not deceive Time, not even rosy lips and cheeks
The harvest is in the field;
Love doesn't just change for hours and weeks,
But bring it to the end of the loss.
If this is wrong and I think so,
I never wrote, and no one loved me.

Don't let me marry the real feelings
Identify barriers. The combination is not love
What does change if one finds the change
Or pulls the knife to remove.
Oh no! This is a permanent sign
It looks at storms and never stops;
It's a star for every star,
The value of which is unknown, though its length is taken into account.
Love is not the fool of time, though the pink lips and cats
His pose comes with a standing court.
Love does not change with these days, hours, and weeks.
But it also brings them to death.
If it is a mistake and I am justified
I never wrote or loved anyone.

I'm not going to a real-minded wedding
Accept the obstacles. Love is not love
Changes when change is detected,
Or curl with the removal to remove.
Oh no! It is always a clear sign
He watches trials, never staggers;
There is a star in every wandering bark,
Who knows the value, but takes his height.
Rosie's lips and cheeks, but love is not the idiot of time
He enters the compass of his curved sickle;
Love does not change with its short hours and weeks,
But it bears the brink of destruction.
If this is a mistake and it is proven against me,
I never write and no one ever likes it.

Let me be a true marriage
Acknowledge obstacles. Love is not love
What changes when change is found
Or bend to get away from the curve.
Oh no! It is constantly fixed
It looks like a storm and never shakes;
This is a star on all the shells of the stick,
Whose value is unknown, even if its height is taken.
Love is not a fool of time, even with pink lips and cheeks
Its curve falls inside the compass;
Love does not change with its short hours and weeks
But bring him to the brink of judgment.
If this is a mistake and I'm proven
I never write and no man likes it.

MACHINE TRANSLATION:
TOWARD A GLOBAL REFUGEE IDIOLECT

Automated algorithmic language translation has rapidly evolved over the past decade. But despite major improvements from advanced machine learning and artificial intelligence algorithms trained on diverse languages and large datasets, these translation tools remain limited and relatively partial. In the hands of a poet the imperfection of machine translation—an imperfection that cannot be removed because imperfection is central to the project of translation—can become a tool for creativity. Take, for example, the output of a translation with grammatically incorrect diction, an "error" in machine translation, which would be then expected to be "fixed" by users, with these fixes informing future iterations of the translation program. I'm interested in the language before the fix. This recovery of language sometimes happens when translated words and phrases resonate with the human poet as "right" for reasons the programmer of such translation tools would see as "wrong." Recovery of language works as a form of rediscovery in these moments in which we are presented with defamilarized language that is strange yet distantly familiar.

I propose that these errors of translation could be read not as signs of the impossibility of machine translation, but rather as a bridge between languages, striking unintended emotional chords and producing by way of error artistic depictions of life, especially as codified by the multi-lingual reader. Such readers are always translating, always code-switching. Through their uses of language, they feel their way through multiple worlds of meanings and possible variants. This results in a poetics of confusion that resists the kind of correction that might normalize the language in favor of a written English that corresponds to the way people actually speak English.

I use machine translation tools to recover what could be called the global refugee idiolect. It is global because what I am describing is a post-colonial phenomenon in which speakers routinely cross borders linguistically; it is an idiolect, a habitual discourse belonging to an individual speaker, because it bears the traces of their fugitive relation to idioms and their confrontation with multiple languages that function as the resources by which they create cultural bridges through language. Authentic poetic language for the multi-lingual reader needs to nod to several languages and codes at once in order to be realistic, such as glimpses of a phrase half in one language and half in another, or diction correctly translated from one language combined with syntax left over from the first. These moments allow a global idiom to emerge.

· While studying creative writing as an undergraduate, I learned about the OuLiPo and found this group fascinating. I experimented with spam erasures, making a sort of found poetry out of unsolicited bulk emails. Spam email may have started out as just massively addressed advertisements, but by the early 2000s it had become more adversarial as it morphed into a machine-written text designed to combat another automated reader: the spam-filtering algorithms used by email providers. I initially worked with these sorts of emails because certain phrases jumped out at me while I scanned my inbox. Later, I found that spam emails were much easier to edit than poetry coming straight from my brain through my fingers.

Though these spam erasures were "my poems," in the classroom and in conversation, I was careful to make the distinction that I did not write them. A machine wrote them. I just edited them and called them poems, asking the reader to consider them as such. My spam poems were like erasure poems but instead of using an established or canonical text as the source text, I used the machine-generated and filter-defying gibberish of spam email as my jumping-off point. Later I would write a series of erasures using *Moby-Dick*. After that, the source for an erasure that I made would be the code that took Apollo 11 to the moon. These were heavily researched undertakings. Years before I attempted such projects, I found my first doorway into experimenting with erasure poetry through daily spam emails I found in my inbox. Working with these texts was fun, especially when the grammatical errors were strange or beautiful.

Around that same time, when Digital Equipment Corporation's AltaVista was the search engine everyone used, Digital made freely available an online translation tool called Babelfish. I eagerly used this to translate my poems (written in English) into Spanish and then back into English again. This generated phrases like "eggs expensive," which seemed apt when talking about eggs I'd eaten at a hotel in Mexico. Translating into Spanish and then back into English was a way of seeing my poems the way my Cuban grandmother (hereafter referred to as Abuela) might see or think through my poetry. I heard her voice in my head, and I decided to keep what other people might consider errors in the diction produced by this double machine translation. There was something familiar about the word ordering of Spanish transliterated into English and the process felt essential to the poetic voice I was cultivating.

My father was born in Cuba; he and his family left in his childhood, just after the Bay of Pigs invasion. His English is New York through and through, but his mother's English is mostly Spanish translated into English and shot through with Spanish words. Presenting her voice poetically to an English-speaking audience felt too problematic, and as I didn't have the language to talk about that yet, I began a series of poems inspired by machine translation: all my early workshop poems went into Spanish and back again. Some old lines remained almost unchanged, but new ideas emerged from the unlikeliest of places. I also went back to conversations with Abuela for poetic inspiration. She would correct my Spanish by repeating it back to me in English. Bears protect the town? she'd ask, when what I'd meant to convey is that my town hosts a bear sanctuary. Her words stayed with me and became the title of a poem: "Bears Protect the Town."

My poetry blends the voices of Abuela and my family in Queens, New York with my newer friends and neighbors in New Hampshire. Overhearing a neighbor use language in a novel way, I plug it into my computer and see what machine translation can make of it. English to Spanish and back again, or even down a third language road, incorporating German perhaps, since there are no online dictionaries for the dialect of German that was my mother's first language. My machine-aided method often produces something totally different than the poems I set out to write, yet I wind up someplace arguably more real, more sincere, in putting my poems through these revisionary paces. Surely it's not just my Abuela that speaks this way, or my own way of hearing the world around me: America is a nation of immigrants, yet there aren't many Abuelas in books speaking in what I now think of as a global refugee idiolect. This will not always be the case.

To write my Abuela as a character who speaks perfect English would have been dishonest; the phrases wouldn't have sounded like her. But to have her speaking Spanish in my writing wouldn't have made sense either, because that's not entirely how she speaks to me. Nothing seemed as realistic as the awkwardness and ambiguity I read in spam emails that accidentally hit on some moments of familiar confusion. From there it was a short leap to machine translation to generate some confusion of my own.

Certain mistakes feel familiar and recognizable while certain perfectly executed discourses feel foreign. I sought to bumble my way through spam and machine noise with an aim toward something authentic, not distant and ironic. This is the opposite of what critic Jennifer Ashton reads in the work of the poets she argues are engaged in "The New Sincerity" movement, in which, according to Ashton, a poet's use of digital tools leads to a point of alienated disconnection:

Through the poem's capacity to index rather than depict or represent the self, the subjective contents of that self—whether we're thinking of the poet or of the people whose speech acts are deposited on the Google servers—are effectively disconnected from everything that does reside within the representational registers of the poem.

What if Ashton's "speech acts" are actually gems, though, poetic sparks that do not have to disconnect at all but help us go more deeply into the poetry of the digital world and discover something there that unites us? How do fragmented gems produce connection? Ashton's separation of the "the poet" from "the people whose speech acts are deposited on Google servers" is a false distinction. Ashton's reading builds the case for an alienated poetics, reflecting the idea that a digital world makes us more separate, even from what could conceivably be our own "speech acts." What if the poet saw the digital world, mapped the landscapes of the Internet and designated the poet's place in it as a site of coming-together rather than estrangement?

Unlike the disaffected poets Ashton writes about, what I'm going for is a poetics of reconnection. The way language is overheard seems to be some of the most critical ways we understand, especially in early childhood. Ashton addresses this relationship within the digital:

> It's worth pursuing the implications of identifying the practice of Googling with overhearing, because this invocation of overhearing matches up with a very specific and longstanding fantasy of poetic creation, one that concerns not only the nature of the material that constitutes the poem itself, but even more important, the poet's relation to that material and the reader's relation to what the poet has done with it.

I'm interested in the work and process that the poets of "The New Sincerity" are engaged with, but my own digital-poetic explorations are quite different. I want to use technology to make contact with my lost (grand)mother tongues and to recover authentic relations by way of computer mediation.

"Flarf" poetry uses technology in order to produce a deflated presence. While I seek signal, Flarf amplifies the noise. While Flarf reimagines the literary landscape as a pastiche of robotic nonsense, Ashton's understanding of machine-aided and machine generated poetry points in the exact opposite direction of my project:

> By removing the last vestiges of creativity (in Flarf it's the manipulation of the source material), word-for-word transcription and the boredom it produces begin to look like a much more powerful means of achieving the same effects as Flarf. That is, of achieving a kind of "presence" of the self in the work, even as the emotional and experiential particularities of that self—everything that makes it a self—are rendered completely irrelevant to the work.

Ashton reads these poems as getting away from emotion and experience, all that I understand to make up human selves, while I seek to use machine translation in my poetry to draw together the multiple selves that a blending of three distinct languages can engender.

My third language is what my mother grew up speaking: a critically endangered language called Gottscheerish. A dialect of German, Gottscheerish comes from Gottschee, a place in what-is-now-Slovenia, where my mother's family lived for hundreds of years and fled during World War II. More Gottscheers live now in the transnational community established in Ridgewood, Queens than anywhere else in the world.

Because my mother and her mother and her grandmother all spoke Gottscheerish and my father and his family spoke Cuban Spanish and we all spoke English at different levels of fluency, I'm attracted to defamiliarized and broken language. Machines will produce fewer "broken" translations as algorithms get better and knowledgeable users correct and modify translations, at least with tools like Google Translate. Rita Raley, a cultural theorist of machine translation, writes:

> Ambiguities are created in the movement from one language to another, certainly, but the rationale of machine translation is to send a signal with a clear, decipherable message. It follows, then, that the primary discursive sites for machine translation are the weather, finance, and the news, all of which affect neutrality and require only a functionally basic semantic accuracy.

Raley contends that we are moving toward a more global English. Machine translation at its best would clear up all ambiguity, yet language can never be a mere "clear, decipherable message." The drive for monolingualism and the dream of pure legibility is ideological; it flattens difference in favor of a single discourse that is marked by uneven access. There is an appeal to what Raley writes of as a "signal with a clear, decipherable message," yet there is also a cost—especially to poets who may find themselves lit up by spam and prefer messy renderings to clean translation.

The ambiguity created by machine translation is precisely what I love about it. Correctness organizes thoughts while ambiguity scrambles them. The pleasure of figuring something out far outweighs the negotiable victory of comprehension. Poets are constantly searching not only for the right words but for the words that fit together like a puzzle to reveal something greater, the code words that comprise the language-game, mirroring social use of language but with the knowledge that meanings change over time, that language is not fixed, but dynamic. Perhaps for poets the greatest pleasure of ambiguity rests in the hope that some readers will understand their intention while others will veer off wildly into an interpretation all their own.

So what might it mean when Raley argues that within machine translations and machine languages we can see evidence of a move toward a global English because code and code comments are oriented in that direction? Why does code skew toward the English-speaking user? Is this clarity that we are working towards just a digital colonialism, and if so, do we risk losing the sincerity of ambiguity and the poetic veracity of trans-language mistakes?

Machine languages—I learned to code in a language called Python—are far less complicated than natural languages. As Alexander Galloway writes, code is "the first language that actually does what it says," and when code is written perfectly non-compliance is not an option. A machine has no choice but to perform a perfectly executed command. Which is to say, when one gives code commands to a machine, if their syntactical moves are made correctly, the machine will respond exactly how it is commanded to respond. One may find however, that making computers do exactly what one tells them to do is not authentic to their human experience, which is blurry and multiple.

Now if I write a perfect poem, what happens? I don't know, I haven't written one yet. It's nothing like what happens if you write perfect code, as Galloway understands it, in which the rules are the rules are the rules. The syntactical structures are difficult until you master them, and from there it's like putting words on a page to make a sentence, a phrase, or a line in a poem. While a line in a poem might beseech the reader, a line of code commands the machine.

My own process includes machines but isn't machine exclusive. I have no interest in attempting to erase myself or my own voice from the process and I would like to see more of that process-based and/or machine-aided art enrich the landscape of creative writing. This book uses Shakespeare's Sonnet 116 to demonstrate that. Here's the poem I'm using:

Let me not to the marriage of true minds
Admit impediments. Love is not love
Which alters when it alteration finds,
Or bends with the remover to remove.
O no! it is an ever-fixed mark
That looks on tempests and is never shaken;
It is the star to every wand'ring bark,
Whose worth's unknown, although his height be taken.
Love's not Time's fool, though rosy lips and cheeks
Within his bending sickle's compass come;
Love alters not with his brief hours and weeks,

But bears it out even to the edge of doom.
If this be error and upon me prov'd,
I never writ, nor no man ever lov'd.

I chose this poem because I love it. It was read aloud as part of my wedding ceremony. Most native speakers of English do not completely understand this poem, in part because it is not written in contemporary English. But they're comfortable with their confusion. Perhaps that's the way many people feel about poetry. That's part of the reason why I like this example—it will confuse machines too, because of the non-standard, non-contemporary English, words like *bark* (meaning ship, not the outermost layer of a tree trunk) and the apostrophes in *wand'ring, prov'd* and *lov'd*. I like that the machine reading won't be able to interpret or try to reproduce the iambics but perhaps make a new kind of music.

I also like messing with this poem because it is so well-known, so canonical, that the mistakes and confusions of translation feel almost personal. When Jen Bervin erased most of Shakespeare's sonnets in her 2004 book of poetry *Nets*, it felt liberating. This book walks the path she created with that work.

The poems in this book are made entirely through machine translation of Shakespeare's Sonnet 116, with each poem's translation pathway as the title. We begin in English, move to another language, then another, then perhaps a third, and then back to English. Like this:

English: Let me not to the marriage of true minds
English → Hindi: मुझे सच्चे मन से शादी न करने दें

Hindi → Yoroba: Ma je ki n fe yin
Yoroba → English: Let me love you

In this way, the poem moves, the poem lives, it is reincarnated, re-produced, misunderstood, mistaken. In creating human-made art and machine-made art that embraces noise, mistakes, and uncertainty, we get closer to the lived experience of all the people who have been displaced, will be displaced, and have inherited linguistic displacement. Such a shift could enable the amplification of the real signal and noise of our own lives and culture, might include rather than exclude new speakers, create new media, and the discovery of a new poetics.

CODE OPTIONS

You can replicate what I did in this book simply by putting the text of a poem into Google Translate and translating it from English to another target language and then back to English. If you are interested in something more technical, here are some options using Python and a few popular packages that you might try. The first uses TextBlob and the thing you need to know here is that TextBlob will soon end support for translation. Still, this method is a good way to think through the experiment. The others use the googletrans package, which also uses the Google Translate API but does so in a different way.

```python
#!/usr/bin/env python
# coding: utf-8

# Experiment 116
#
# Rena J. Mosteirin
# rena.j.mosteirin@gmail.com
# 10/20/2020

# For examples of using TextBlob, see Nick Montfort's
# Exploratory Programming for the Arts and Humanities
# (MIT Press).

from textblob import TextBlob
```

```python
# The following list of lists defines the paths taken for
# each iteration
# of translation. I start with English for completeness.
# These codes
# are later translated back to language names with the
# LANGUAGES dictionary
# below.

language_paths = [
    ['en', 'de', 'ku', 'en'],
    ['en', 'ca', 'ht', 'en'],
    ['en', 'fr', 'sn', 'en'],
    ['en', 'sl', 'eu', 'en'],
    ['en', 'es', 'ja', 'en'],
    ['en', 'mi', 'la', 'en'],
    ['en', 'ha', 'gl', 'en'],
    ['en', 'ne', 'lb', 'km', 'en'],
    ['en', 'el', 'haw', 'en'],
    ['en', 'sv', 'th', 'en'],
    ['en', 'zh-tw', 'bs', 'en'],
    ['en', 'gd', 'yi', 'en'],
    ['en', 'ps', 'sm', 'en'],
    ['en', 'cy', 'fy', 'en'],
    ['en', 'ko', 'ga', 'en'],
    ['en', 'pl', 'tl', 'en'],
    ['en', 'it', 'jw', 'tt', 'en'],
    ['en', 'af', 'hmn', 'en'],
    ['en', 'co', 'mk', 'en'],
    ['en', 'ceb', 'zu', 'be', 'en'],
    ['en', 'rw', 'ms', 'en'],
    ['en', 'hy', 'am', 'en'],
    ['en', 'sw', 'he', 'en'],
    ['en', 'sr', 'vi', 'en'],
    ['en', 'hi', 'yo', 'en'],
    ['en', 'sm', 'uk', 'te', 'en'],
    ['en', 'st', 'lv', 'la', 'en'],
    ['en', 'gu', 'eo', 'en'],
    ['en', 'lo', 'uz', 'en'],
    ['en', 'su', 'is', 'ig', 'en'],
    ['en', 'id', 'ta', 'nl', 'en'],
    ['en', 'or', 'no', 'en'],
    ['en', 'ru', 'xh', 'en']
```

```
]

LANGUAGES = {
    'af': 'afrikaans',
    'sq': 'albanian',
    'am': 'amharic',
    'ar': 'arabic',
    'hy': 'armenian',
    'az': 'azerbaijani',
    'eu': 'basque',
    'be': 'belarusian',
    'bn': 'bengali',
    'bs': 'bosnian',
    'bg': 'bulgarian',
    'ca': 'catalan',
    'ceb': 'cebuano',
    'ny': 'chichewa',
    'zh-cn': 'chinese (simplified)',
    'zh-tw': 'chinese (traditional)',
    'co': 'corsican',
    'hr': 'croatian',
    'cs': 'czech',
    'da': 'danish',
    'nl': 'dutch',
    'en': 'english',
    'eo': 'esperanto',
    'et': 'estonian',
    'tl': 'filipino',
    'fi': 'finnish',
    'fr': 'french',
    'fy': 'frisian',
    'gl': 'galician',
    'ka': 'georgian',
    'de': 'german',
    'el': 'greek',
    'gu': 'gujarati',
    'ht': 'haitian creole',
    'ha': 'hausa',
    'haw': 'hawaiian',
    'iw': 'hebrew',
    'he': 'hebrew',
    'hi': 'hindi',
```

```
'hmn':  'hmong',
'hu':  'hungarian',
'is':  'icelandic',
'ig':  'igbo',
'id':  'indonesian',
'ga':  'irish',
'it':  'italian',
'ja':  'japanese',
'jw':  'javanese',
'kn':  'kannada',
'kk':  'kazakh',
'km':  'khmer',
'ko':  'korean',
'ku':  'kurdish (kurmanji)',
'ky':  'kyrgyz',
'lo':  'lao',
'la':  'latin',
'lv':  'latvian',
'lt':  'lithuanian',
'lb':  'luxembourgish',
'mk':  'macedonian',
'mg':  'malagasy',
'ms':  'malay',
'ml':  'malayalam',
'mt':  'maltese',
'mi':  'maori',
'mr':  'marathi',
'mn':  'mongolian',
'my':  'myanmar (burmese)',
'ne':  'nepali',
'no':  'norwegian',
'or':  'odia',
'ps':  'pashto',
'fa':  'persian',
'pl':  'polish',
'pt':  'portuguese',
'pa':  'punjabi',
'ro':  'romanian',
'ru':  'russian',
'rw':  'kinyarwanda',
'sm':  'samoan',
'gd':  'scots gaelic',
```

```
    'sr': 'serbian',
    'st': 'sesotho',
    'sn': 'shona',
    'sd': 'sindhi',
    'si': 'sinhala',
    'sk': 'slovak',
    'sl': 'slovenian',
    'so': 'somali',
    'es': 'spanish',
    'su': 'sundanese',
    'sw': 'swahili',
    'sv': 'swedish',
    'tg': 'tajik',
    'ta': 'tamil',
    'te': 'telugu',
    'th': 'thai',
    'tr': 'turkish',
    'tt': 'tatar',
    'uk': 'ukrainian',
    'ur': 'urdu',
    'ug': 'uyghur',
    'uz': 'uzbek',
    'vi': 'vietnamese',
    'cy': 'welsh',
    'xh': 'xhosa',
    'yi': 'yiddish',
    'yo': 'yoruba',
    'zu': 'zulu',
}

sonnet_116 = """Let me not to the marriage of true minds
Admit impediments. Love is not love
Which alters when it alteration finds,
Or bends with the remover to remove.
O no! it is an ever-fixed mark
That looks on tempests and is never shaken;
It is the star to every wand'ring bark,
Whose worth's unknown, although his height be taken.
Love's not Time's fool, though rosy lips and cheeks
Within his bending sickle's compass come;
Love alters not with his brief hours and weeks,
But bears it out even to the edge of doom.
```

```
If this be error and upon me prov'd,
I never writ, nor no man ever lov'd."""


for path in language_paths:

    traversed_path=list()
    for i,l in enumerate(path):

        # On each iteration we should add language name,
        # "translated" from
        # the language code using the above LANGUAGES
        # dictionary object, to
        # our path.

        traversed_path.append(LANGUAGES[l].capitalize())

        # Since we are beginning with the English
        # language version of the
        # sonnet, on our first iteration we want to create
        # a TextBlob object
        # from the poem.

        if i == 0 and l == "en":
            sonnet = TextBlob(sonnet_116)

        # For each subsequent iteration, we'll request
        # a Google Translate
        # translation from the source to target language.

        else:
        # source language is the previous item in our
        # path array
            source = path[i - 1]

        # target language is our present position in
        # the path list
            target = l

        # Translate! The "from" parameter is optional
        # and while
```

```python
        # Google Translate seems quite (perhaps especially)
        # capable of
        # detecting the language of text that it has
        # produced, we will
        # be explicit to make sure that the correct
        # language is used.

        sonnet = sonnet.translate(from_lang=source,
                to=target)

    print("\n→ ")     # Copy and paste the → from the Web
                      # or use --> instead.
    print(" → ".join(traversed_path))
    print(" →")
    print(sonnet)


#!/usr/bin/env python
# coding: utf-8
#
# Experiment 116
#
# Use googletrans package and use all Google Translate
# supported languages
#
# Rena J. Mosteirin
# rena.j.mosteirin@gmail.com
# 11/19/2020


# import and configure the Translator
from googletrans import Translator
translator = Translator()


sonnet_116 = """Let me not to the marriage of true minds
Admit impediments. Love is not love
Which alters when it alteration finds,
Or bends with the remover to remove.
O no! it is an ever-fixed mark
That looks on tempests and is never shaken;
It is the star to every wand'ring bark,
Whose worth's unknown, although his height be taken.
Love's not Time's fool, though rosy lips and cheeks
Within his bending sickle's compass come;
```

Love alters not with his brief hours and weeks,
But bears it out even to the edge of doom.
If this be error and upon me prov'd,
I never writ, nor no man ever lov'd."""

```
language_paths = [
 ['de', 'ku', 'en'],
 ['ca', 'ht', 'en'],
 ['fr', 'sn', 'en'],
 ['sl', 'eu', 'en'],
 ['es', 'ja', 'en'],
 ['mi', 'la', 'en'],
 ['ha', 'gl', 'en'],
 ['ne', 'lb', 'km', 'en'],
 ['el', 'haw', 'en'],
 ['sv', 'th', 'en'],
 ['zh-TW', 'bs', 'en'],
 ['gd', 'yi', 'en'],
 ['ps', 'sm', 'en'],
 ['cy', 'fy', 'en'],
 ['ko', 'ga', 'en'],
 ['pl', 'tl', 'en'],
 ['it', 'jw', 'tt', 'en'],
 ['af', 'hmn', 'en'],
 ['co', 'mk', 'en'],
 ['ceb', 'zu', 'be', 'en'],
 ['rw', 'ms', 'en'],
 ['hy', 'am', 'en'],
 ['sw', 'iw', 'en'],
 ['sr', 'vi', 'en'],
 ['hi', 'yo', 'en'],
 ['sm', 'uk', 'te', 'en'],
 ['st', 'lv', 'la', 'en'],
 ['gu', 'eo', 'en'],
 ['lo', 'uz', 'en'],
 ['ur', 'tk', 'en'],
 ['su', 'is', 'ig', 'en'],
 ['id', 'ta', 'nl', 'en'],
 ['or', 'no', 'en'],
 ['my', 'pa', 'en'],
 ['ru', 'xh', 'en'],
 ['sq', 'ug', 'en'],
```

```
    ['ar', 'hu', 'en'],
    ['so', 'az', 'en'],
    ['fa', 'ny', 'en'],
    ['kn', 'pt', 'en'],
    ['ky', 'bn', 'en'],
    ['bg', 'mn', 'en'],
    ['tr', 'lt', 'en'],
    ['da', 'tt', 'en'],
    ['cs', 'kk', 'mr', 'en'],
    ['mt', 'tg', 'en'],
    ['si', 'sk', 'en'],
    ['mg', 'hr', 'en'],
    ['et', 'sd', 'en'],
    ['ml', 'ro', 'en'],
    ['fi', 'ka', 'en']
]
```

LANGUAGES = {'af':'Afrikaans', 'sq':'Albanian', 'am':'Amharic',
'ar':'Arabic', 'hy':'Armenian', 'az':'Azerbaijani',
'eu':'Basque', 'be':'Belarusian', 'bn':'Bengali',
'bs':'Bosnian', 'bg':'Bulgarian', 'ca':'Catalan',
'ceb':'Cebuano', 'ny':'Chichewa', 'zh-CN':'Chinese', 'zh-
TW':'Chinese (Traditional)', 'co':'Corsican', 'hr':'Croatian',
'cs':'Czech','da':'Danish', 'nl':'Dutch', 'en':'English',
'eo':'Esperanto', 'et':'Estonian', 'tl':'Filipino','fi':'Finnish',
'fr':'French', 'fy':'Frisian', 'gl':'Galician', 'ka':'Georgian',
'de':'German', 'el':'Greek', 'gu':'Gujarati', 'ht':'Haitian
Creole', 'ha':'Hausa', 'haw':'Hawaiian', 'iw':'Hebrew',
'hi':'Hindi', 'hmn':'Hmong', 'hu':'Hungarian', 'is':'Icelandic',
'ig':'Igbo', 'id':'Indonesian', 'ga':'Irish', 'it':'Italian',
'ja':'Japanese', 'jw':'Javanese', 'kn':'Kannada', 'kk':'Kazakh',
'km':'Khmer', 'ko':'Korean', 'ku':'Kurdish (Kurmanji)',
'ky':'Kyrgyz', 'lo':'Lao', 'la':'Latin', 'lv':'Latvian',
'lt':'Lithuanian', 'lb':'Luxembourgish', 'mk':'Macedonian',
'mg':'Malagasy', 'ms':'Malay', 'ml':'Malayalam', 'mt':'Maltese',
'mi':'Maori', 'mr':'Marathi', 'mn':'Mongolian', 'my':'Myanmar
(Burmese)','ne':'Nepali', 'no':'Norwegian', 'or':'Odia (Oriya)',
'ps':'Pashto', 'fa':'Persian', 'pl':'Polish', 'pt':'Portuguese',
'pa':'Punjabi', 'ro':'Romanian', 'ru':'Russian', 'rw':'Kinya
rwanda','sm':'Samoan', 'gd':'Scots Gaelic', 'sr':'Serbian',
'st':'Sesotho', 'sn':'Shona', 'sd':'Sindhi', 'si':'Sinhala',
'sk':'Slovak', 'sl':'Slovenian', 'so':'Somali', 'es':'Spanish',

```
        'su':'Sundanese', 'sw':'Swahili', 'sv':'Swedish', 'tg':'Tajik',
        'ta':'Tamil', 'te':'Telugu', 'tk':'Turkmen','th':'Thai',
        'tr':'Turkish', 'tt':'Tatar','uk':'Ukrainian', 'ur':'Urdu',
        'ug':'Uyghur', 'uz':'Uzbek', 'vi':'Vietnamese', 'cy':'Welsh',
        'xh':'Xhosa', 'yi':'Yiddish', 'yo':'Yoruba', 'zu':'Zulu'}

for path in language_paths:
    traversed_path=list()
    for i,l in enumerate(path):

        # On each iteration we should add language name,
        # "translated" from
        # the language code using the above LANGUAGES
        # dictionary object, to
        # our path
        # traversed_path.append(LANGUAGES[l])

        # On first iteration, we will be translating
        # from English
        if i == 0:
            sonnet = sonnet_116

        # For each subsequent iteration, we'll request
        # a Google Translate
        # translation from the source to target langauge.
        else:
        # source language is the previous item in
        # our path array
        source = path[i - 1]

        # target language is our present position in
        # the path array
        target = l

        # Translate!
        sonnet = translator.translate(sonnet,
        dest=target).text

        # On conclusion of the path, display our route and
        # the final
        # translated sonnet
```

```
      print("\n→ ")     # Copy and paste the → from the Web
      # or use --> instead.
      print(" → ".join(traversed_path))
      print(" →\n")
      print(sonnet)

# !/usr/bin/env python
# coding: utf-8

# Experiment 116: lc_distance.py
#
# Rena J. Mosteirin
# rena.j.mosteirin@gmail.com
# 11/15/2020


# Use googletrans package for translation
from googletrans import Translator
translator = Translator()

# distance metric: vocabulary frequency
# cosine similarity distance should be fine here
from sklearn.feature_extraction import text
from sklearn.metrics.pairwise import cosine_similarity
import numpy as np

# initializes Scikit-Learn's CountVectorizer
vectorizer = text.CountVectorizer(input='content',
                                  lowercase='true')


# The get_distance function takes a single parameter,
# the target
# language code. The function vectorizes the original
# English-language
# sonnet, translates the sonnet to the target language
# and then back to
# English. The resulting text is the vectorized using Count
# Vectorizer and
# then the cosine similarity is calculated using
# Scikit-Learn's
# cosine_similarity pairwise distance metric.
```

```
def get_distance(lc):
    tt = translator.translate(translator.translate(sonnet_116,
        dest=lc).text,
        dest="en").text
    counts = vectorizer.fit_transform([sonnet_116,tt])
    dist = cosine_similarity(counts[1][0].toarray(),
        counts[0][0].toarray())[0][0]
    return(dist)



# These are the supported languages for Google Translate
LANGUAGES = {'af':'Afrikaans', 'sq':'Albanian', 'am':'Amharic',
'ar':'Arabic', 'hy':'Armenian', 'az':'Azerbaijani','eu':'B
asque', 'be':'Belarusian', 'bn':'Bengali', 'bs':'Bosnian',
'bg':'Bulgarian', 'ca':'Catalan', 'ceb':'Cebuano',
'ny':'Chichewa','zh-CN':'Chinese', 'co':'Corsican',
'hr':'Croatian', 'cs':'Czech','da':'Danish', 'nl':'Dutch',
'en':'English', 'eo':'Esperanto', 'et':'Estonian',
'tl':'Filipino','fi':'Finnish', 'fr':'French', 'fy':'Frisian',
'gl':'Galician', 'ka':'Georgian', 'de':'German',
'el':'Greek', 'gu':'Gujarati', 'ht':'Haitian Creole',
'ha':'Hausa', 'haw':'Hawaiian', 'iw':'Hebrew','hi':'Hindi',
'hmn':'Hmong', 'hu':'Hungarian', 'is':'Icelandic',
'ig':'Igbo', 'id':'Indonesian', 'ga':'Irish', 'it':'Italian',
'ja':'Japanese', 'jw':'Javanese', 'kn':'Kannada',
'kk':'Kazakh','km':'Khmer', 'ko':'Korean', 'ku':'Kurdish (Kur-
manji)', 'ky':'Kyrgyz','lo':'Lao', 'la':'Latin', 'lv':'Latvian',
'lt':'Lithuanian','lb':'Luxembourgish', 'mk':'Macedonian',
'mg':'Malagasy','ms':'Malay', 'ml':'Malayalam', 'mt':'Maltese',
'mi':'Maori', 'mr':'Marathi', 'mn':'Mongolian','my':'Myanmar
(Burmese)','ne':'Nepali', 'no':'Norwegian', 'or':'Odia (Oriya)',
'ps':'Pashto','fa':'Persian', 'pl':'Polish', 'pt':'Portuguese',
'pa':'Punjabi', 'ro':'Romanian', 'ru':'Russian', 'sm':'Samoan',
'gd':'Scots Gaelic', 'sr':'Serbian', 'st':'Sesotho',
'sn':'Shona', 'sd':'Sindhi', si':'Sinhala', 'sk':'Slovak',
'sl':'Slovenian', 'so':'Somali', 'es':'Spanish', 'su':'Sundanese',
'sw':'Swahili','sv':'Swedish', 'tg':'Tajik', 'ta':'Tamil',
'te':'Telugu','th':'Thai', 'tr':'Turkish', 'uk':'Ukrainian',
'ur':'Urdu', 'ug':'Uyghur', 'uz':'Uzbek', 'vi':'Vietnamese',
'cy':'Welsh', 'xh':'Xhosa', 'yi':'Yiddish', 'yo':'Yoruba',
'zu':'Zulu'}
```

```python
sonnet_116 = """"Let me not to the marriage of true minds
Admit impediments. Love is not love
Which alters when it alteration finds,
Or bends with the remover to remove.
O no! it is an ever-fixed mark
That looks on tempests and is never shaken;
It is the star to every wand'ring bark,
Whose worth's unknown, although his height be taken.
Love's not Time's fool, though rosy lips and cheeks
Within his bending sickle's compass come;
Love alters not with his brief hours and weeks,
But bears it out even to the edge of doom.
If this be error and upon me prov'd,
I never writ, nor no man ever lov'd.""""


# for each non-English language in the LANGUAGES dictionary,
# calculate distance using get_distance function

lang_dist = dict()
for lc in LANGUAGES.keys():
    if lc != "en":
        lang_dist[lc] = get_distance(lc)

# The following will sort cosine similarity distances from
# the original English-language Sonnet 116 and plot with a
# simple distance chart scaled for easy viewing. The higher
# the value, the closer the resulting poem is to the
# original English language.

for l, v in sorted(lang_dist.items(), key=lambda x:
x[1],reverse=True):
    sv = int((v * 100) / 2)
    print("{0:6s} {1:6f} {2}".format(l,np.round(v,4),'#'*sv))
```

```
no     0.828700 ###################################
da     0.826500 ###################################
es     0.824300 ###################################
cy     0.819400 ##################################
yi     0.818100 ##################################
mk     0.812000 ##################################
```

```
sv     0.811400  ####################################
st     0.809600  ####################################
ga     0.800900  ####################################
fi     0.799000  ####################################
ne     0.798500  ####################################
bg     0.798200  ####################################
lv     0.794800  ####################################
ht     0.794600  ####################################
vi     0.794500  ####################################
ps     0.792500  ####################################
nl     0.791700  ####################################
zu     0.791700  ####################################
kn     0.791300  ####################################
ur     0.790600  ####################################
af     0.788000  ####################################
el     0.787400  ####################################
sq     0.787400  ####################################
lt     0.786200  ####################################
cs     0.785200  ####################################
mt     0.785100  ####################################
co     0.784900  ####################################
eo     0.784600  ####################################
fr     0.779500  ####################################
it     0.779200  ####################################
sl     0.778000  ####################################
hu     0.777300  ####################################
xh     0.777100  ####################################
de     0.776900  ####################################
ku     0.775500  ####################################
id     0.772400  ####################################
bn     0.771800  ####################################
bs     0.771600  ####################################
ja     0.771200  ####################################
zh-CN  0.769000  ####################################
gu     0.767500  ####################################
mn     0.766500  ####################################
gl     0.766400  ####################################
km     0.766100  ####################################
th     0.765600  ####################################
fy     0.765500  ####################################
gd     0.764700  ####################################
pt     0.763000  ####################################
```

```
hi     0.762800  ###################################
hr     0.762700  ###################################
tl     0.762300  ###################################
te     0.760800  ###################################
lb     0.760700  ###################################
ru     0.759700  ###################################
is     0.758500  ###################################
hmn    0.758300  ###################################
tr     0.758100  ###################################
or     0.757200  ###################################
pa     0.756800  ###################################
tg     0.756500  ###################################
jw     0.756300  ###################################
ml     0.755900  ###################################
lo     0.753200  ###################################
si     0.753200  ###################################
ka     0.751900  ###################################
mr     0.751500  ###################################
sr     0.751200  ###################################
su     0.748600  ###################################
hy     0.748100  ###################################
ca     0.748000  ###################################
fa     0.747500  ###################################
ta     0.747400  ###################################
ro     0.745600  ###################################
sw     0.745100  ###################################
my     0.744300  ###################################
iw     0.743500  ###################################
yo     0.741800  ###################################
uz     0.741500  ###################################
ar     0.740100  ###################################
ceb    0.739800  ##################################
ko     0.738900  ##################################
ms     0.737700  ##################################
be     0.736600  ##################################
sk     0.733900  ##################################
sm     0.730900  ##################################
eu     0.730500  ##################################
sn     0.725000  ##################################
pl     0.723200  ##################################
az     0.718900  #################################
kk     0.717500  #################################
```

```
sd    0.714900  ###############################
ny    0.714600  ###############################
am    0.712500  ###############################
ug    0.709600  ###############################
et    0.708100  ###############################
mg    0.706800  ###############################
so    0.706300  ###############################
mi    0.705800  ###############################
ha    0.704400  ###############################
uk    0.703500  ###############################
ky    0.695600  ##############################
ig    0.691000  ##############################
haw   0.677100  #############################
la    0.666900  #############################
```

REFERENCES

Ashton, Jennifer. "Sincerity and the Second Person: Lyric After Language Poetry" *Interval(le)s* II.2-III.1 (Fall 2008/Winter 2009).

Bervin, Jen. *Nets*. Brooklyn: Ugly Duckling Presse, 2004.

Galloway, Alexander R. *Protocol: How Control Exists after Decentralization*. Cambridge: MIT Press, 2006.

Montfort, Nick. *Exploratory Programming for the Arts and Humanities*. 2nd edition. Cambridge: MIT Press, 2021.

Raley, Rita. "Machine Translation and Global English." *The Yale Journal of Criticism* 16, no. 2 (2003): 291-313.

ACKNOWLEDGMENTS

Nick Montfort, I've long admired your poetics and still can't get over the good fortune of getting to work on this book with you. I am deeply grateful to Tim Roberts and Counterpath Press and the authors in the Using Electricity series, for lighting up my thinking.

This book began as a lecture for the Bennington Writing Seminars MFA program and is indebted to the support of my outstanding Bennington mentors; Mark Wunderlich, April Bernard, Carmen Gimenez-Smith and Major Jackson. Jenny Boully's notes and encouragement on the earliest versions of this work kept me pushing and digging and dreaming of this book. Megan Culhane Galbraith, your generosity has allowed me to stay connected to the Bennington community, and I am deeply grateful. Hannah Howard, Jessica Silvester and Frances Greathead, can we please get together and dance all night?

As this work developed I've been teaching for the MALS program at Dartmouth College and learning how to be a teacher from Don Pease, Wole Ojurongbe and Barbara Kreiger. Many thanks to the first professor who gave me the tools to explore the vast digital landscape, Thomas H. Cormen.

As this material grew, I was very grateful for generous feedback from four writers I deeply admire; J. Hope Stein, Britt Peterson,

Chris Prentice and Reb Siegel. To my sister-horses Kristina Rapua-no and Vassiki Chauhan, when I want to feel brave, I pretend to be you.

James E. Dobson, my first reader/collaborator/husband/best friend, this has been one hell of a year, hasn't it? When the pandemic was breaking my heart, you took me out late-winter rowing in your homemade wooden boat and as we pushed through the slush you chanted *frozen margs, frozen margs* until I laughed. For this and for all your translations of grief and loss into humor and joy, I thank you.

This book is for my parents and their parents. When I talk about my multi-lingual family in this book I'm thinking most about my father's mother, Martha Josefa Bozza Bontempo Mosteirin; my mother's mother, Maria Wenda; and my great-grandmother Helen Schmuck. These three women were hugely influential in my early language development, and they loved me very much when I was a child. It wasn't until I was grown that I could begin to imagine what their lives were really like. By this I mean, all three of them were forced to flee situations of hideous violence. They landed in Queens, New York, lived as refugees, raised children in a foreign land, and did the best they could. They learned English but they didn't pray in English. They lived in the U.S. but they never loved it. They dreamed of going home and woke knowing that no meaningful version of their homes existed anymore. This book is for them.